Close to Home Uncut

**Other Close to Home Books
by John McPherson**

One Step Closer to Home
Home: The Final Frontier
The Honeymoon Is Over
The Silence of the Lamberts
Striking Close to Home
The Close to Home Survival Guide

Treasury Collections
Close to Home Unplugged

Close to Home Uncut

a Close to Home Collection
by John McPherson

ZondervanPublishingHouse
Grand Rapids, Michigan

A Division of HarperCollinsPublishers

Library of Congress Catalog Card Number: 00-103480

Michael—This one's for you.

Shortly into the date, Evan triggers
Kelly's personal security alarm.

"And what could be worse than ground-in dirt?!
Yooouuu guessed it! Pet stains!"

"Okay, Mr. Frawley . . . severe sinus congestion."

"My husband said send the bill to
the New York Jets."

"Isn't it clever? The legs pop out
when it's done cooking!"

"Either our dual airbags have a wildlife theme,
or a deer just jumped through the window."

To help them cope, many stay-at-home moms are turning to the new life-size T. Berry Brazelton doll.

"Your brakes are all set, Mrs. Helfer. However, our insurance company requires that you wear this protective suit throughout our ninety-day warranty period."

"You're just more affected by Novocain than most people, Mr. Cromley. You should regain full use of your legs in a day or two."

"Mrs. Stalnaker?! Neil Haggerty, Unity National Health Insurance. Put down the cheesecake now, or we'll double your premium!"

"Okay, now!"

Vicky loved to take guests on tours of Dave's unfinished projects.

"Don't look at me! I don't have the slightest
idea how they got out there!"

"To help you better understand this good choles-
terol/bad cholesterol thing, Nurse Bowman and
Nurse Strickling are going to do a little skit for you."

"Oh yeah, I meant to tell you about that.
The icemaker is screwed up."

"Andy! Start rewrapping 'em now!
Mom and Dad just pulled in the driveway!"

"Personally, I think Ray is a little too into this mouse extermination project."

"How long ago did she develop this appetite for throw rugs?"

Gary demonstrates his new no-shovel driveway.

19

EMERGENCY
WAITING AREA

"I always thought 'Do not open until Christmas' was just an expression."

"I must have said it three times: 'Don't forget to pick up some toilet paper when you're out!'"

For those really frantic diaper changes,
Rita relied on her foot-activated wipes dispenser.

"I don't have time for *games*, Mr. Watkins!"

"It's the annual holiday letter from the Mumfords.
Lisa graduated magna cum laude from Cornell.
Marge is taking a pottery course. Stan built a
thirty-two-foot yacht out of scrap lumber.
Who the heck are the Mumfords?"

"If there are any among us who know of some rea-
son why Todd and Janet should not be joined in
marriage, let them speak now or . . ."

Just twenty-six hours after closing on their new home,
Pam and Gary Winslow would discover why they were
able to buy it for forty percent below market value.

When shaking the presents just won't cut it.

Having discovered that she's out of pasta and with dinner guests arriving in twenty minutes, Jean is forced to use the kids' macaroni necklaces.

"According to our background check, you missed seven days of kindergarten due to illness. That puts you in our high-risk category."

"Oh, look at that! First a lawn mower and now a snow shovel! How about a big thank you for your father, Marty?!"

"We've already had calls from two pro soccer teams and an international water skiing show."

"I'm sorry, sir, but frequent flier miles can be used only on non-holiday weekdays that are divisible by nine."

"Well, it figures! I spent all morning waxing the stairs and in two seconds you've got 'em all scuffed up again!"

**Thanks to her new academic camouflage,
Lisa was rarely called on in class.**

"Look, honey, I don't mean to pressure you, but if the baby isn't born within the next fifty-three minutes, we can kiss that 2000 tax write-off goodbye."

"Any of you who are here regarding the Johnny Space Ranger Action Laser Gun, I can take you over here."

As Frank finished his six-hour shoveling job,
he suddenly heard the evil cry he'd witnessed
so many times before.

"Muffin has been transferred to a
veterinary hospital for the criminally insane."

"Every year right about now the building settles a
couple of inches. The only thing we can figure
is that it has something to do with the
weight gain of tenants after the holidays."

"Jerry suffers from Seasonal Affective Disorder Syndrome."

"Thank you, Erik, for that vivid
presentation on meteor showers."

The hazard of rolling over in a bed with flannel
sheets while wearing a flannel nightgown.

Dave opens up his birthday gift from Mamie.

Twenty-seven years of finding Phil's toenail clippings
lying around the house culminated in one glorious
act of revenge for Donna.

"Okay, Doug, somebody's in the bathroom.
Let's take it into a dive!"

"At last, paint sample chips big enough to actually
give you a feel for how the color will look!"

"It's steak sauce! Just our way of keeping a sense of humor around here!"

"The instructions say we have to soak the spare tire in warm water for two hours until it swells to its usable size."

"Okay, Mrs. Wertman, your installation is all set. Let's run through the operation. Do you, by any chance, have a watermelon?"

"That's the last time we shop at Everything for a Buck."

The latest in child-care products: fortune diapers.

"I told you it was a stupid idea to make an
obscene gesture at a road sanding truck."

"The guy up in 18-B is a fireman."

Burger Baron ups the ante in the lucrative kids' meal market.

"Ma'am, for your sake, I hope you're giving birth within the next twenty minutes."

"You don't suppose this has anything to do with you sending back the first three entrees?"

"Jerry, the chimney sweep wants to talk to you about his estimate."

On their third date, Pam finds out if Alan is a cat person.

"If you're planning on videotaping the birth, we're gonna need twenty minutes to touch up our makeup."

Operating on the same principle as an electric pencil sharpener, Tina's new Insta-Shave can safely shave both of her legs in just fifteen seconds.

"Those of you who ate the chicken at the Fowler-Doherty wedding can come with me. And we'd appreciate it if you three bridesmaids would stop chanting, 'Kill the caterer!'"

44

"Ma'am, I've been appointed spokesperson for the other passengers. We're prepared to offer you $637.82 to take a later flight."

Focusing too hard on his snowplow technique, first-time skier Ernie Dunlop makes a tragic navigational error.

"Order anything from our dessert cart and get this 'Joy of Liposuction' video absolutely free."

"I can't believe that nun on the third floor actually tried to catch it!"

"It says in gigantic red letters on page one of the manual: 'DO NOT USE THE SNOWBLOWER ON GRAVEL SURFACES!'"

"Carol, your computer has a very serious virus. We can't risk having it spread to the other PCs. You know this is for the best. Please step aside."

An unwavering truth of grocery shopping with a toddler: Your child *will* throw a tantrum, and it will invariably happen when your minister, pediatrician, and mother-in-law are walking by.

A growing service industry: chaperones for people who met on the Internet.

"Before you go, Mr. Gertman, we'd like you to fill out this customer satisfaction card to let us know how we can better serve you."

"Okay, Mr. Hayworth, it looks as if you'll be flying in economy class with us today."

With cold and flu season in high gear, Brenda wisely carried her sneeze shield whenever she went out in public.

"For heaven's sake! *That* certainly was a sensitive car alarm!"

"We know you don't have any children,
Mrs. Hillard, but to pass your driver's test,
you need to be able to drive in all conditions."

Cornered by a mob of angry wives, mailman
Virgil Wingate is forced to hand over every
copy of the *Sports Illustrated* swimsuit issue.

"I'm tellin' ya, Sheila, it's not easy living with a perfectionist."

Although he thought their argument had been settled at breakfast, Jim sensed that Sally had some unresolved issues.

"Really? I look familiar? You probably recognize me from the airline's expose on '60 Minutes' last week!"

"That price includes a two-year supply of mice."

"Okay, when Mom comes out to get the mail,
grab her as hard as you can!"

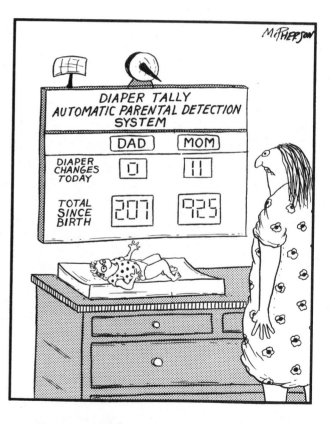

Drew's date with Christine takes a turn for the worse.

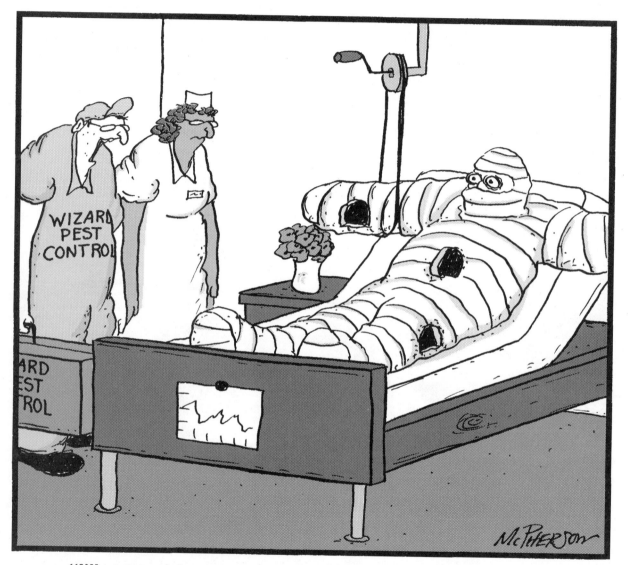

"I'll start with conventional mousetraps, and if they don't take care of them, we'll have to fumigate."

"George! Great news! I found my ring!
I didn't wash it down the sink after all!
It was on my dresser the whole time!"

Thanks to his phenomenal accuracy,
Frank hadn't had a parking ticket in years.

"Just make sure the pacemaker is on the
proper setting and you'll be fine, Mr. Lusk."

The agony of enrolling your child in a
hyper-illness-sensitive day-care center.

"Yep, that's definitely Tina babysitting for the Winslows! Those back-stabbers stole our sitter, knowing full well that tonight is our anniversary!"

"I'm not quite sure what's going on here, but I don't think it bodes well for our luggage."

"How many times do I have to tell you not to slam the door?!
When your father comes in from shoveling,
he's going to have something to say about this!"

"Mr. Stekson, we are very busy people. Do you want the finest hair-replacement procedure available or not?"

How tax software should work.

"Look out. I'm gonna get a running start at it."

"Really? I'll have to try that. Could I have your name and address? My lawyer suggests that I keep a list of everyone who gives me unsolicited advice just in case there's a problem."

Hoping to inject some life into an incredibly dull date, Meredith pulls out her defibrillator paddles.

The Lubermans prepare for Willie's third birthday party.

"Well? How did your consultation at the acupressurist go?"

"It was the cutest thing! Jordan felt so bad about leaving his marbles on the stairs, he made this cast for his dad out of Legos!"

Determined to keep heating bills to a minimum, Ken had the contractor install a placebo thermostat in the new house.

"Hey, Annette! Put this on! He should be coming to any minute!"

"Will you shut up about how ironic this is?!"

"This is our new Romance Enhancer shower curtain. It makes everything look twenty-five percent slimmer."

By rigging their fitness machines to give exaggerated calorie readouts, the Atlantis Health Club increased its membership by sixty-five percent.

Just three days after **Burt** bought his snowblower, the Wagners perfected their act.

Glenda reminds Ted not to leave his dirty laundry lying around the house.

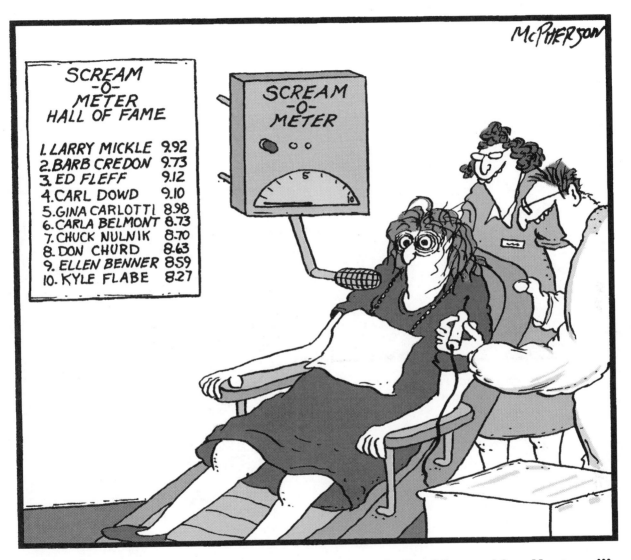

"All right! 8.65! You just made it into the hall of fame, Mrs. Kestner!"

As a public service, many radio stations
now provide winter illness reports.

Hoping to instill more pride in academics,
Oakfield High devised report card T-shirts.

Dinnertime for working parents is reduced to its most basic form.

Midway through the interview, Wayne decides to see how well the applicant handles stress.

"Whoa! Up fourteen pounds since November! What'd you do? Get a job at a doughnut shop?!"

"Okay, here he comes. Let me do the talking."

"It's regular plasma. We just color it green
in honor of St. Patrick's Day."

"Vince, you won't believe what I found at a rummage sale!"

"Dave claims he's totally earthquake-proofed the house now, like that's a major concern here in Cleveland."

"Mrs. Brackett, how would you like to be in the *Guinness Book of World Records?*"

Suspecting that just such a word problem might be on the algebra midterm, Gary came prepared.

"Oh, that's nothing! It's just there in the unlikely event that we have to make an emergency water landing!"

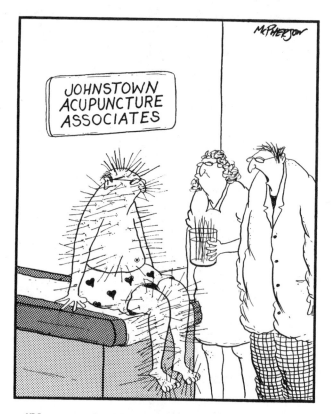

"You gotta be kidding! Your back *still* hurts?!"

"Well, the pest guy's truck is still here.
Let's hope he's having some luck getting rid
of whatever's been making that hideous
scratching noise in the walls."

"Folks, we're very sorry about this little accident. Please accept this voucher for one complimentary appetizer on any Monday in April."

"It's just like they always say—a new car depreciates thirty percent the second you drive it off the lot."

"Okay, young man, that does it! When we get home you are having a time-out!"

"The manual says it needs 187 'D' batteries."

"Those are twenty percent off."

84

After months of gathering dust, the Norsteens'
$1,500 treadmill is finally put to use.

"The insurance company is right. We've got
its basic policy that covers only illnesses
that begin with the letters A through G."

"Well, you have to admit it is nice to have more leg room."

"Cool! I didn't know Mike Tyson had a Web site!"

"Okay, Mr. Feldman. You're all prepped for surgery."

The Norstadts devise a subtle plan to force their
newly returned adult son to move out.

"He learned how to climb out,
so we greased the crib."

Tollbooth operator Zena Calhoun stumbles onto a gold mine.

Determined to increase productivity, management finds a way for employees to work straight through lunch.

Showdown at the Westgate Rest Plaza.

"Just so we don't have a repeat of this morning's fiasco, I superglued a tack to the snooze button."

Having discovered a faint pulse in his lab frog,
Doug quickly began CPR.

Parentonics.

"Hey, Phil, bring the net. This woman just picked little Jerry, the orphan with the deformed claw that all the other lobsters pick on."

"You're not going to weasel out of buying me a Jacuzzi this easily!"

"Woooo! We got one! We killed an ant! He was a wily little bugger, too! We've been trackin' him for nearly two hours!"

In an effort to emphasize both physical fitness and academics, officials at Westbury High devised aerobic algebra.

"Could you please eat that in the break room? My dietitian says that secondhand snacks aren't good for me."

"Aw, shucks. That suit didn't fit either, huh?"

A busy mother of two, Cindy relied on her
hydraulically operated Mother's Helping Hands®.

"What? Oh, geez, no. The baby's
not due until September. We just
got our sonogram results today."

"Uh, Bruce, Derek. Come on, guys, you're supposed to be checking for drugs and weapons."

"I'm trying to remember if I've seen this one."

"Dr. Franey is in the Bahamas for two weeks, but we can visit his Web site."

"*That* was the sound of a custom-made graphite 5-iron going through a ten-horsepower chipper! Let's listen to a titanium driver! Or are you *finally* in the mood to wallpaper the kitchen?!"

"Whoa! Not so fast, hotshot! The librarian says you're not graduating until you return the copy of *Green Eggs and Ham* you've had out since March of 1989!"

Before taking her out, Charlene's dates were required to take a brief vocabulary lesson.

"What kind of glue works best on bones? Heh, heh! Daryl, my boy, you *do* come up with some imaginative questions."

Like many parents, the Gelmans found themselves caught in a cycle of trying to outdo the previous year's birthday party.

"We're conducting a study on the healing power of humor. As Boppy performs for you, let us know the precise moment that you feel the kidney stone pass."

"Oh, all right. I guess we could stop at *one more* house to 'ask directions' before we deliver the check."

"Oh, that. The landlord lives downstairs. This is his way of verifying that we don't have pets."

"I *did* call the builder. He said it's normal for a new house to settle a bit and that he'll give us a twenty-five percent discount on all caulking supplies."

ATTENTION PASSENGERS OF NORTHMONT FLIGHT 403. WE ARE EXPERIENCING SOME DIFFICULTIES WITH OUR BAGGAGE-RETURN SYSTEM. WE HOPE TO HAVE THIS PROBLEM CORRECTED MOMENTARILY.

"Hey, you! I told you yesterday to stay out of here!
You want me to call the cops?"

"Are you the genius who left a bag of lollipops in the backpack?"

"I developed a dependency on treadmills over the winter."

"Bud's Garage is seven miles ahead.
'Two stars. Great soap dispensers, attractive
tilework. But toilet paper supply is unreliable
and flies can be horrible.'"

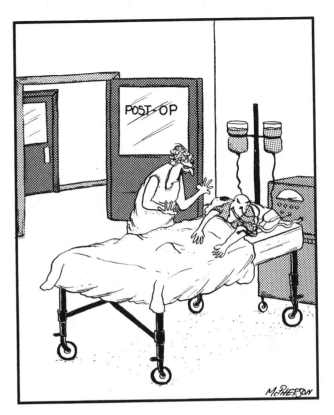

"Oh, George! How sweet! They left
a mint on your pillow!"

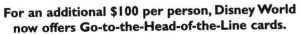
For an additional $100 per person, Disney World
now offers Go-to-the-Head-of-the-Line cards.

"Aw, come on, Ken! If we've got to lay off people, at least let us have some fun with it!"

"The time has come to buy our son a pair of headphones!"

"Will you relax?! Trust me. This shortcut is going to shave
twenty minutes off our trip."

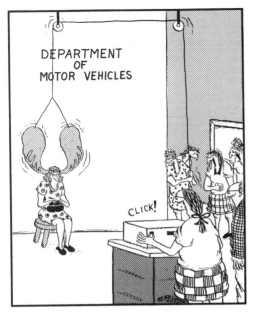

"Okay, ma'am! You should receive
your license in three weeks."

"Everyone ... ah, ha, ha! ... get out of here! We've got
a ... ha, ha ... leak in our ... hee! ... laughing-gas tank!
Oooo-weee! Ha, ha! Go on, you scamps! Shoo!"

"And this indicator here is called the 'Queas-O-
Meter.' If the needle dips into the red zone, get off
the apparatus immediately and head to the bathroom."

"It's very simple, Diane. When you leave on a date,
you punch out on the time clock.
When you get home, you punch in."

"Ma'am, we're filming an episode of 'Real Adventures of the Highway Patrol.' Even though all we've got you on is speeding, would you mind making a break for the woods and letting Randy here tackle you?"

"It's just a little challenge we like to offer newlyweds. If you can jump over the ribbon, you get to keep our bathrobes."

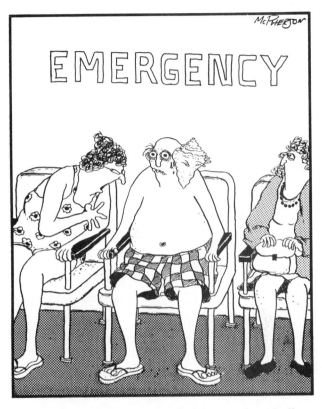

"I told him three times, 'Don't put that shell
up to your ear! It's still got a crab in it!'
So what does he do? . . . "

"For heaven's sake, Andrew!
That is a very nasty splinter!"

"Unfortunately, there will be no cost-of-living
increases this year. Instead, you'll receive this
coupon book containing $1,500 in savings,
plus this brochure titled 'How to Refine
Your Own Heating Oil.'"

"If I hear 'The flight leaves in thirty-five minutes,'
'You should've checked the oil level,' or
'non-refundable tickets' one more time . . . "

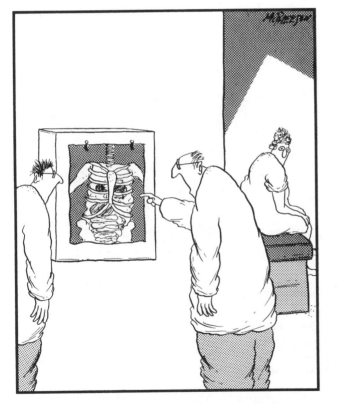

"Well, there's the problem. That squiggly
gizmo is splurting glop all over that
gross-looking doohickey."

"Anytime one of the kids gets an illness we cross it off. When we complete a row, Ed and I are going to Tahiti for three weeks."

"Oh, for heaven's sake! It wasn't a bee after all! It was just a piece of fuzz from my skirt!"

"If anyone tries to look at someone else's answers and turns his or her head a mere three inches . . . TIMBER!"

"Could you be a dear and tell me whether or not I packed my blowdryer?"

"The wedding ends at 2:30. Give us about a minute to throw some rice on them ourselves, and then you come diving down and nail 'em!"

"Okay, so I lied a little about its appearance. But think of the advantages of this home! 1. No painting! 2. No washing windows! 3...."

"Jenkins! Could I see you in my office for a moment?!"

"Joyce, write this down in Mr. Cutler's file:
'thump . . . thump-thump . . . thumpety-thump . . .
boink.'"

"I'm collecting for Larry Shumski's get-well gift.
Which donation should I put you down for?
Homeboy, $25; nodding acquaintance, $10;
or tightwad scum, $5?"

"To help you monitor your progress, we make a plaster cast of every member's posterior once a month."

"Relax! It's not a real tattoo! I just want to see the look on my mother-in-law's face when she arrives tomorrow."

Life with a compulsive mileage calculator.

"Now that I've officially graduated, I'd just like to say, 'Mr. Ogstead, I'm the one who dumped the bucket of tapeworms down your shirt during that biology movie three years ago!'"

"Sasha's listening, Mrs. McGinnis.
Oh, she just gave a big smile. Look at that
tail go! She's so happy, she's drooling."

Management unveils its new formula
for determining comp time.

"Really? Three weeks? Brandon started sleeping
twelve hours at just two weeks, which made it a lot
easier for me to get back into my step aerobics class!"

"There's the key to the ladies' room, and while
you're in there could you do me a favor
and set this behind the toilet?"

Every year during finals, Mr. Garmon flushes out several cheaters with the same bluff.

"That suit comes with ten pairs of cellulite-filtering sunglasses for you to give to your friends."

"For the 100th time, I'm sorry I bent your new driver
while trying to unclog the toilet!"

"Holy smokes, that was close! We're probably the only people in history who've seen an entire herd of mountain goats faint!"

To help parents identify their child's cry, many play centers have hired professional linguists.

"Let me guess—3 a.m., Home Shopping
Network?"

"Okay, let's see ... peas, meatloaf, potatoes, and
milk. We'll say $3.50. Oh, wait, you had seconds,
didn't you, Brad?"

"Mikey, turn off Road Runner and try to help Daddy! Tell Daddy what buttons to push to fix a general fault protection error/hard drive failure!"

"Help me play a little prank on my husband. Start walking away with these while exclaiming that you can't believe you bought a set of new graphite clubs for ten bucks."

"Aunt Delia! Uncle Buzz! How nice of you to stop by unexpectedly! Unfortunately, we've got the measles! Can you believe it? All of us!"

"What on earth? Frank, look out!"

"I don't care if you emptied it ahead of time!
Who in their right mind would put a litter box
in a dishwasher?!"

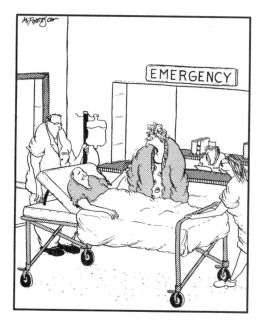

"For the fourth time, Hal, no, I won't forget
to get the parking stub validated!"

"Thanks for another nice haircut, and sorry
I made that comment about you looking heavier.
I think it's just that dress making you look pudgy."